How to Draw the Life and Times of
# Andrew Johnson

Ryan P. Randolph

The Rosen Publishing Group's
PowerKids Press™
New York

*To my dad*

Published in 2006 by The Rosen Publishing Group, Inc.
29 East 21st Street, New York, NY 10010

First Edition

Editor: Daryl Heller
Layout Design: Albert B. Hanner

Illustrations: All illustrations by Holly Cefrey.
Photo Credits: pp. 4, 12, 26 © Bettmann/Corbis; pp. 7, 8, 9, 18, 20, 24, 28 Library of Congress;
p. 10 © Corbis; p. 14 © Medford Historical Society Collection/Corbis; p. 16 Library of Congress
Geography and Map Division; p. 22 © Alinari Archives/Corbis.

Library of Congress Cataloging-in-Publication Data

Randolph, Ryan P., 1975–
    How to draw the life and times of Andrew Johnson / Ryan P. Randolph.— 1st ed.
        p. cm. — (A kid's guide to drawing the presidents of the United States of America)
    Includes index.
    ISBN 1-4042-2994-9 (library binding)
    1. Johnson, Andrew, 1808–1875—Juvenile literature. 2. Presidents—United States—Biography—
Juvenile literature. 3. Drawing—Technique—Juvenile literature. I. Title. II. Series.

    E667.R25 2006
    973.8'1'092—dc22

                                                                    2004027118

Manufactured in the United States of America

# Contents

# Meet Andrew Johnson

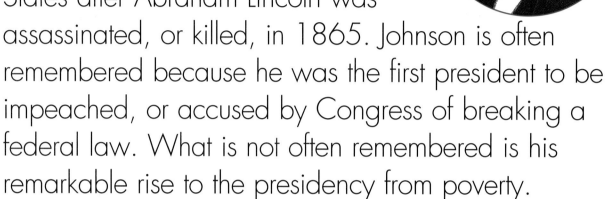

Andrew Johnson became the seventeenth president of the United States after Abraham Lincoln was assassinated, or killed, in 1865. Johnson is often remembered because he was the first president to be impeached, or accused by Congress of breaking a federal law. What is not often remembered is his remarkable rise to the presidency from poverty.

Andrew Johnson was born in Raleigh, North Carolina, on December 29, 1808. His parents, Jacob and Mary Johnson, were quite poor. Although Johnson never attended school, he trained with an established tailor in North Carolina. Johnson later opened his own tailor shop in Greeneville, Tennessee.

In 1829, Johnson was elected as a town representative, his first political post. He then became a representative in state government in 1835. From the beginning of his political career, Johnson was known as a forceful public speaker. Johnson continued to rise and between 1843 and 1857, he was elected a U.S. congressman, the governor of Tennessee, and a U.S. senator.

As a politician Johnson protected the rights of poor white people. He also believed in the importance of the U.S. Constitution and sought to keep the United States together when the issue of slavery was in danger of breaking it apart. On the eve of the Civil War, when all the Southern states, including Tennessee, had voted to secede, or withdraw, from the United States, Johnson refused to join them. Johnson was considered a traitor to the South. However, his defense of the Union earned him Abraham Lincoln's respect and the nomination as vice president in the 1864 presidential election.

You will need the following supplies to draw the life and times of Andrew Johnson:

✓ A sketch pad   ✓ An eraser   ✓ A pencil   ✓ A ruler

These are some of the shapes and drawing terms you need to know:

| | | | |
|---|---|---|---|
| Horizontal Line | —— | Squiggly Line | ∿ |
| Oval | ⬭ | Trapezoid | ⏢ |
| Rectangle | ▭ | Triangle | △ |
| Shading | ▓ | Vertical Line | │ |
| Slanted Line | / | Wavy Line | ∼ |

# The Seventeenth President

When Andrew Johnson became president in 1865, his biggest task was how to bring the Southern states back into the Union after the Civil War. This process of rebuilding the South and protecting the rights of the newly freed African Americans was known as Reconstruction. Johnson felt it best to reestablish relationships with the Southern states quickly. His plan provided a general amnesty, or forgiveness, to the Southern soldiers and politicians who had fought against the Union. Johnson encouraged the Southern states to adopt the Thirteenth Amendment, which abolished, or banned, slavery in the United States.

Northern congressmen, who were known as Radical Republicans, thought Johnson's Reconstruction plan was too kind to the South. Many Southern states had already established Black Codes, or laws that limited the former slaves' rights. The Radical Republicans wanted the newly freed slaves to have the rights of U.S. citizens. Andrew Johnson vetoed, or refused to approve, the laws created by the Radical Republicans.

President Johnson's opposition to the Radical Republicans would lead to his impeachment in 1868. This *Harper's Weekly* print from 1868 shows Johnson's impeachment trial, which was held in the U.S. Senate. President Johnson chose not to attend the trial.

# Andrew Johnson's Tennessee

Andrew Johnson's brick home in Greeneville, Tennessee, is part of a national park that honors Andrew Johnson.

Map of the United States of America

Although Andrew Johnson was born in North Carolina, he moved to Tennessee as a young man and spent much of his adult life in Greeneville, Tennessee. Today people can visit the Andrew Johnson National Historic Site, located in Greeneville. This 17-acre (7 ha) park consists of several separate properties, which include a visitor center, a museum, and Andrew Johnson's tailor shop. Nearby is an early home where Johnson lived when not at work in his tailor shop.

A few blocks away from these buildings is a larger house called Homestead. Johnson began living in this house in 1851, after he had met with success in both politics and business. The house is furnished with the Johnsons' furniture. Andrew Johnson's grave site is also part of the park. The burial ground contains a marble monument in honor of Johnson. The 1878 monument is topped with an eagle and is carved with a Bible and the U.S. Constitution. On the monument are the words, "His faith in the people never wavered." This means he never lost his belief in the people of the United States.

This is the parlor inside Homestead, Johnson's house shown on the facing page. The painting on the wall was created when Johnson was in the U.S. Senate. The ivory basket to the left of the couch was given to Johnson by Queen Emma of Hawaii. The table on the right was a gift from the Irish people.

# A Tennessee Tailor

At an early age Andrew Johnson and his brother William were apprenticed to a tailor named James Selby. In exchange for working in his tailor shop, Selby gave the boys food and shelter, and taught them how to make and repair clothes. A few years later, Johnson sought his fortune in the western regions of the United States. In 1826, he and his family arrived in Greeneville, Tennessee, where Johnson opened a tailor shop, which is shown above. In May 1827, Johnson married Eliza McCardle. The couple was happily married and had five children.

Johnson had learned some basic reading and writing skills as Selby's apprentice. Eliza continued his education. Johnson's tailor shop was so successful that he soon had other tailors working for him. The shop also became a place where townspeople debated, or discussed, the issues of the day. Johnson's strong speaking style gained him popularity with the workingmen in town. In 1829, he was elected as a village alderman.

**1** To begin drawing Johnson's tailor shop, draw a large rectangle. Inside this rectangle draw two smaller rectangles side by side as shown. The left inside rectangle is the smallest.

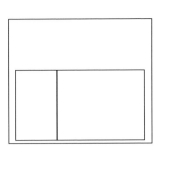

**2** Draw a vertical line on either side of the vertical line the two rectangles share. Add a rectangle above these lines. Draw two slanting shapes along the top and slanted lines on the bottom.

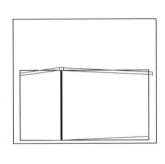

**3** Erase the rectangular guides you made in step 1. Draw three vertical lines on the cabin's left side. Add a small vertical line on the end of the slanted shape on the left. Draw a small rectangle at the top. The lines are guides for the chimney.

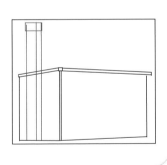

**4** Draw six slanted lines for the roof. Add another line along the base of the cabin. Draw three small rectangles for the windows and the door. The rectangles for the windows are smaller than the rectangle for the door.

**5** Erase extra lines. Draw the chimney as shown. Add rectangular shapes to the windows and the door. Draw a rectangle over the door for the sign. Add lines for the window shutters. On the side of the house, draw the lines and shapes.

**6** Erase the guides for the chimney. Add the words "A. JOHNSON TAILOR" to the sign above the door. Draw lines inside the door, windows, and shutters as shown. Add vertical and horizontal lines and shapes along the bottom and the side of the cabin.

**7** Add horizontal lines across the front and the side of the tailor shop. Note how the lines are not seen when they pass behind the chimney. The lines also end at the windows and door. Add more shapes and slanted lines to the bottom of the cabin.

**8** Finish by shading the tailor shop. The chimney and the bottom portion of the cabin are the darkest. Shade the roof and front of the cabin a bit lighter. The inside of the house and the windows are shaded as well.

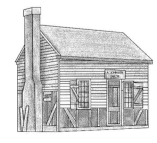

# Five-Term U.S. Congressman and the Homestead Movement

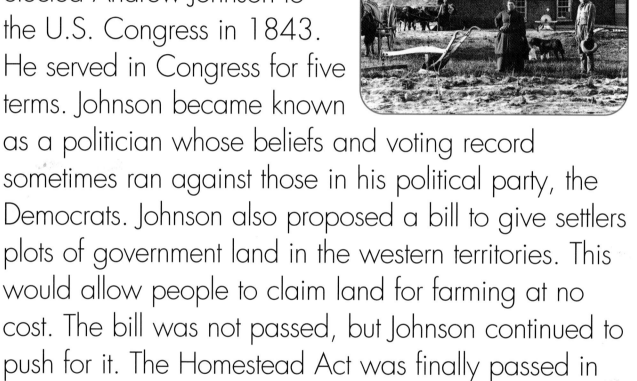

After he had served in a variety of political posts, the people of Tennessee elected Andrew Johnson to the U.S. Congress in 1843. He served in Congress for five terms. Johnson became known as a politician whose beliefs and voting record sometimes ran against those in his political party, the Democrats. Johnson also proposed a bill to give settlers plots of government land in the western territories. This would allow people to claim land for farming at no cost. The bill was not passed, but Johnson continued to push for it. The Homestead Act was finally passed in 1862. Shown above are Homestead Act settlers farming their land in Nebraska around 1870.

Johnson also did not want poor white people to be taxed too heavily. Therefore, he worked to limit the money the government spent. Even though public improvements would help the economy and all people, Johnson did not want poor people to have to pay for these improvements.

**1**

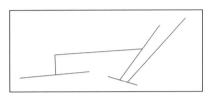

A plow is a farm tool that is used to cut and turn over the soil. To begin drawing a plow, draw a large rectangle. This will be a guide for your drawing.

**2**

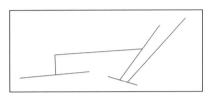

Inside the rectangular guide, draw two long slanted lines on the right for the plow handles. Draw four more lines for the rest of the plow as shown. These guides will help you draw the basic shape of a plow.

**3**

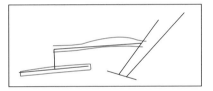

Draw two curved lines around the top guide you just made in step 2 for the top of the plow. Next draw a curved shape around the slanted guideline at the bottom left of the plow.

**4**

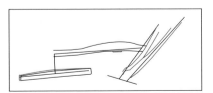

Add lines inside the guides for the handles as shown. Add lines to the bottom left shape as shown. Add a small shape underneath the middle of the plow.

**5**

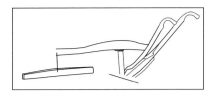

Erase extra guides. Add curved lines to the top of the plow handles. Add more lines to the bottom of the plow handles as shown. Draw two slanted lines underneath the plow, coming from the smaller shape you added in step 4.

**6**

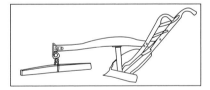

Add curved lines for the chain at the front of the plow. Add slanted lines connecting the handles as shown. Use curved lines and shapes to make the shovel at the bottom of the tool as shown.

**7**

Erase extra lines. Add more shapes to the front of the plow. These shapes include circles, lines, and a small rough rectangular shape. Add small circles for bolts on the plow handles as shown.

**8**

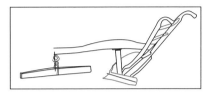

Erase the rectangular guide you made in step 1. Finish by shading the plow.

# Governor of Tennessee

The Democrats did not nominate Johnson to run for Congress in 1852. The 1852 election was won by a candidate from the Whig Party. The Whigs wanted a strong federal government that would raise money through taxes. This money could be used to build U.S. businesses and the economy. Johnson's support of all white men, not just wealthy businessmen, put him at odds with the Whigs. Johnson, like many Democrats, thought individual states should make their own laws. The states, not the federal government, should tax their citizens or choose whether to allow slavery.

Johnson ran for governor of Tennessee in 1853 as a Democrat. He beat the Whig candidate Gustavus A. Henry and took office that October. Johnson served twice as governor, and each term lasted two years. During this time he proposed a school tax bill that improved the school system and public libraries in Tennessee. The poor benefited the most from funding to public schools and libraries. Above is the Tennessee capitol in which Johnson served as governor.

**1** To begin creating the Tennessee capitol, draw a large rectangle. Inside the large rectangle, draw three smaller rectangles. Note the size and how these shapes are set on top of each other.

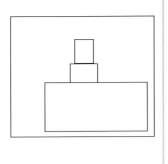

**2** Add a vertical line and four slanted horizontal lines to make the side of the building. Add three slanted lines along the front of the bottom rectangle. Add a vertical line at the right bottom corner.

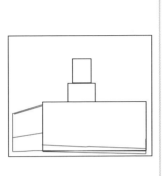

**3** Erase extra lines. Add another rectangle to the bottom rectangle as shown. Add more lines along the left side of the building. These lines include a triangle and slanted lines for the roof, and lines for the building's base.

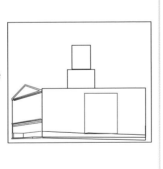

**4** Add lines to the roof area and to the front and side of the building as shown. Add shapes inside the middle and top rectangles using straight and curved lines.

**5** Add more slanted and vertical lines across the side of the building as shown. Add lines to the two shapes you made in step 4. The top shape uses curved lines. The lower shape uses slanted lines.

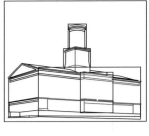

**6** Erase the extra guides. Draw many vertical lines for the columns on the side and front of the building. Draw small rectangles along the bottom of the building. Add the curved shape to the top of the building. Add short vertical lines at the bottom corner sections of the building.

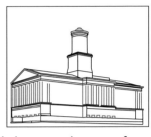

**7** Use rectangles to draw windows on the front of the building and on the tower. Add more columns. Add tops and bottoms to the columns using small shapes. Add a pointed top to the tower using three shapes and a line.

**8** Erase the large rectangle that you made in step 1. Finish by shading the building. The roof, the columns, the base of the building, and the windows are dark. Other parts of the building can be shaded lighter.

# Senator Johnson's Speech Against Secession

Building on his two terms as governor, Johnson was elected to the U.S. Senate from Tennessee in 1857. When he arrived in Washington D.C.,

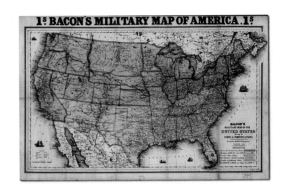

disagreements between representatives from the North and the South over slavery were growing worse. Johnson believed that each state should be able to decide whether to allow slavery within its borders. He also supported the U.S. Constitution and the union of all the states. This position sometimes put him at odds with many southerners, especially wealthy plantation owners in the Democratic Party.

As the presidential election of 1860 approached, the Democratic Party split over the issue of slavery. This division allowed the Republican candidate Abraham Lincoln to win the election. Many southerners felt their states had the right to protect the practice of slavery. After the election many southern states warned they would secede from the Union. Despite his personal support of slavery, on December 18, 1860, Johnson gave a powerful Senate speech defending the Union.

**1**

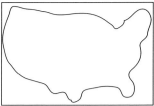

The 1862 U.S. map on the facing page is color coded. States and areas that allowed slavery but stayed in the Union are yellow. Those that did not allow slavery are green. Slave states that seceded, or left the Union, are pink. To begin draw a rectangle. Next draw a wavy line to create an outline.

**2**

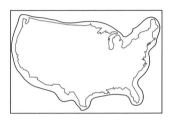

Inside the wavy line you just made in step 1, draw a squiggly line. This will be the shape of the map. Note how the U.S. border curves.

**3**

Erase the guide. On the left side of the map, draw lines for the five western states and territories, which later became U.S. states.

**4**

Add more lines for the next eight states and territories. Notice how some of these areas have a rectangular or square shape.

**5**

Draw more lines to create the group of states in the central area of the United States. You have added 11 more states.

**6**

Next to the lines you just made, draw more squiggly and wavy lines for the outline of the next group of states.

**7**

Draw more states using more squiggly and wavy lines.

**8**

Finish by shading. Code your map by shading the bottom states with slanted lines as shown. Shade the middle states dark. Finally, shade the top states lighter than the middle states as shown.

# Brigadier General and Military Governor of Tennessee

Despite Andrew Johnson's speech, South Carolina seceded from the United States on December 20, 1860. Ten other states soon followed. These 11 states formed the Confederate States of America. Johnson was the only Southern senator to remain true to the Union. The Civil War to bring the states back together began in April 1861. By 1862, Union general Ulysses S. Grant had driven the Confederates from Nashville and other parts of Tennessee. Soon after President Lincoln appointed Johnson to serve as the military governor of Tennessee. Johnson would run the state government with support from the Union army.

Johnson removed all politicians and government workers who approved the secession and appointed people who were faithful to the Union. As Nashville was often in danger of a Confederate attack, Johnson worked to recruit, or hire, new soldiers to the Union army to fight in battles such as the one shown above.

**1** To draw the general and his horse that are shown in the facing image of the 1862 Tennessee battle of Murfreesboro, first draw a rectangle. Next draw a slanted line, two circles, and an oval to begin the horse.

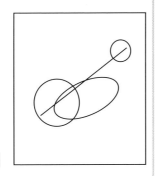

**2** Draw a curved line for the horse's back. Draw slanted lines for the legs. Draw small circles at the ends of the legs for the hooves. Add two lines and an oval to the small top circle to begin drawing the horse's head, neck, and nose.

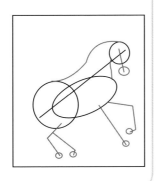

**3** Use the guides to outline the horse's legs. Draw the horse's jaw, forehead, and nose. Add lines for the ears. Use curving lines to make the chest, rear, and tail.

**4** Erase some of the guides for the horse. Add details to the horse's ears, mouth, and hooves. Add two curved lines to the horse's legs. Draw the guides for the head and the body of the rider as shown.

**5** Erase extra lines from the horse. Add details to the horse's hooves and nose. Draw wavy lines for the mane. Use curving lines for the man's hat, cloak, and arm. Draw a circle and two lines for the package behind the rider.

**6** Erase extra lines from the horse's head. Erase the guides for the rider's arms and body. Add lines to the rider's clothing, the package, and the rider's face. Add the rider's leg. Draw the horse's saddle blanket and reins.

**7** Erase extra lines. Draw wavy lines to create details on the rider's clothing. Add more lines to the reins and blanket, and add stirrups for the rider's feet. Add the strap from the blanket to the horse's tail. Add a line to the rider's face.

**8** Erase the rectangle you drew in step 1. Add an eye to the rider's face. Finish by shading the horse and the rider. You have finished your horse and rider from the battle of Murfreesboro. Neither side won this battle.

# Vice President and the Assassination of Abraham Lincoln

In spite of Andrew Johnson's efforts as military governor, Union supporters in Tennessee remained divided as to whether slavery would exist in the state after the war. After touring some Northern states on a February 1863 trip to Washington D.C., Johnson discovered that he was popular with Northern voters.

Hoping to make the most of this popularity, Johnson shifted his position on slavery and supported the 1863 Emancipation Proclamation, which freed slaves in Confederate states. Soon after Abraham Lincoln selected Johnson as his running mate for the 1864 presidential elections.

Lincoln and Johnson won the election and Johnson took office as U.S. vice president in March 1865. However, on April 14, 1865, John Wilkes Booth assassinated President Lincoln at Ford's Theatre in Washington, D.C. A saddened Andrew Johnson was sworn in as president the next day.

**1** The 1864 banner on the facing page celebrated the election victory of Lincoln and Johnson. To begin drawing Lincoln draw an oval. Then draw a smaller oval inside. Draw two slanted lines below this oval.

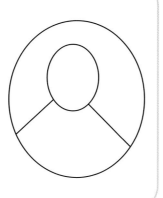

**2** Draw a squiggly line inside the oval guide for the basic shape of President Lincoln's face. Draw two more squiggly lines just below the two slanted guides you made in step 1 for his body.

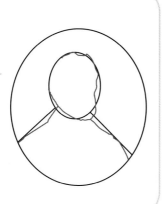

**3** Erase the slanted body guides. Draw four straight lines inside the head as guides for the eyes, nose, and mouth. Add a curved line for the left ear. Add squiggly lines above the head for the hair.

**4** Add a squiggly line inside the face oval for President Abraham Lincoln's beard. Draw four slanted lines to create guides for the jacket collar as shown.

**5** Erase the oval you made for the head in step 1. Add curved lines for the eyes and the nose. Add wavy lines inside the jacket collar. Draw lines for the vest that are just inside the two collar shapes.

**6** Erase guides for the eyes, the nose, and the jacket collar. Add the eyebrows and the hair. Add circles inside the eyes. Draw the mouth. Draw curved lines for the shirt, the bow tie, and the shoulder seam.

**7** Erase the guide for the mouth. Add lines to the ear and to the face as shown. Draw more squiggly lines on the clothing and the bow tie as shown. Add a button on the shirt.

**8** Finish by shading your drawing of Abraham Lincoln. Shade the circles in Lincoln's eyes dark. Shade the folds on the jacket dark. The hair and beard are dark as well.

# The Monroe Doctrine in Mexico

On April 9, 1865, Confederate general Robert E. Lee officially gave up at Appomattox Courthouse, Virginia. The war ended. While

President Andrew Johnson attended to the Reconstruction of the South, he depended on Secretary of State William Seward for advice on how the United States would deal with foreign, or other, countries.

The most serious problem with a foreign country during Johnson's presidency came from France. In 1864, France had conquered part of Mexico and had set up Archduke Maximilian, whose castle is shown above, as the emperor. This was against the 1823 Monroe Doctrine, which said that no European country could invade, or take over, any areas of North America and South America. The United States would consider such actions a danger to national security. Johnson and Seward demanded that the French leave Mexico. In 1867, France withdrew their support of Maximilian. A crisis with France was avoided.

**1**

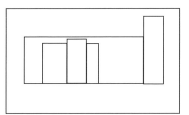

To draw Miramar Castle, which was Maximilian's home before he came to Mexico, draw a large rectangle. Inside the rectangle draw five rectangles as shown.

**2**

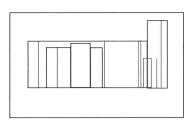

Add seven vertical lines and a small rectangle inside the guides you made in step 1. The rectangle is on the right, on the bottom left edge of the tallest rectangle.

**3**

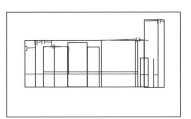

Draw horizontal lines across the rectangles as shown. Add small vertical, horizontal, and slanted lines along the tops of the rectangles.

**4**

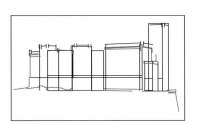

Erase parts of the long horizontal rectangle. Add more slanted, horizontal, and vertical lines to the castle. Draw lines along the bottom of the castle as shown.

**5**

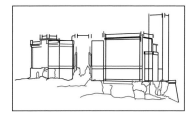

Erase extra lines. Add more squiggly lines along the bottom. Add lines along the sides and top of the castle. Draw the shape for the entranceway.

**6**

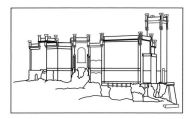

Add detail to the top of the castle. Use lines and shapes to detail the base. Add a large arched window. Draw several curved lines for the tops of other windows.

**7**

Add more detail to the top of the castle. Draw the windows as shown. Most are shaped like arches. Some have extra details. Add a circle on the right tower.

**8**

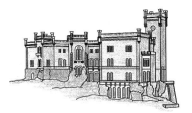

Erase the first rectangle you made in step 1. Finish the drawing by shading the castle. The insides of the windows and the sides of the towers should be shaded darker.

# The Alaska Territory

In addition to preventing a war with France, Seward and Johnson acquired a piece of land. Today that gain is considered a huge accomplishment. In 1867, the Russian government needed money and approached Seward to see if the United States would purchase the Alaska Territory, shown here.

The Russians asked a price of $7.2 million dollars for about 500,000 acres (202,300 ha) of land. The United States wanted to extend its territory west and agreed. Seward created a treaty to complete the purchase, which the Senate approved on April 9, 1867. Johnson approved it on May 28, 1867.

The unpopulated, cold Alaska Territory was much larger than the U.S. state of Texas. Many people did not agree with spending government money on such land, and they called the purchase Seward's Icebox. However, Andrew Johnson's government wisely recognized the value of Alaska's harbors, forests, and its wealth of natural resources, or supplies.

**1** The facing cartoon shows Johnson and Seward carting an ice block that represents Alaska. Begin by drawing a rectangle. Draw another rectangle inside. Draw two circles as shown.

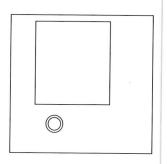

**2** Draw a squiggly line inside the rectangle. Add an oval guide for Johnson's head on the right. Draw slanted lines for the bottom of the cart as shown.

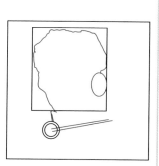

**3** Erase the inner rectangle. Draw an oval for Seward's head on the left. Use slanted lines to draw guides for the men's bodies. Draw slanted lines for the top, side, and legs of the cart as shown.

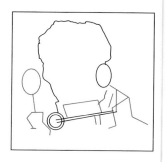

**4** Add lines for their heads and hair. Add guides for Seward's arms. Draw oval guides for the bodies, legs, and feet. Draw a curved line inside the guide you made on the cart. Outline the cart's legs, too.

**5** Erase the head ovals. Add lines to shape the bodies as shown. Add the words "RUSSIAN AMERICA" to the ice and "TREATY" to the cart. Add squiggly lines to the cart and to the ice as shown.

**6** Erase the body guides. Draw the men's hair, arms, and hands. Add lines to the clothes. Draw guides for their eyes and mouths using small slanted lines. Add lines to the ice, cart, and wheel.

**7** Using slanted and wavy lines, add details to the ground, wheel, and men's clothing. Add ropes to the cart. Erase any remaining guides for the men's bodies. Add details to the eyes, nose, and mouth as shown.

**8** Erase the large rectangle that you made in step 1. Erase guides for the face. Finish the cartoon by shading.

# The Impeachment Trial of President Andrew Johnson

After the war the Radical Republicans thought the southern states should be readmitted to the Union only if they protected the rights of newly freed slaves. Congress proposed 29 laws to protect the former slaves and to limit the powers of southern states. Andrew Johnson vetoed, or said no to, every one. Congress overrode Johnson's veto on 15 bills.

In 1867, Congress passed the Tenure of Office Act, hoping to limit Johnson's power. This act said the president could not fire cabinet members without Senate approval. In August 1867, a furious Johnson fired Secretary of War Edwin Stanton. Johnson was impeached for this and stood trial before the Senate. President Johnson's trial was a national event. The president had good lawyers and Congress was divided over whether Johnson was actually guilty of a crime. In the end Johnson was found not guilty by one vote.

**1** Thaddeus Stevens was a congressman who wanted Johnson impeached. To draw Stevens draw a rectangle. Add an oval head guide and guidelines for the body and arms. Draw ovals for the hands.

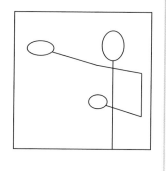

**2** The bottom image on page 26 is from around 1868. It shows Stevens presenting the closing arguments at Johnson's trial. The top image is a ticket to the trial. Add four ovals to the guides you made for the arms in step 1.

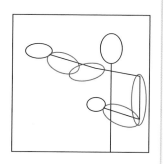

**3** Draw a wavy line for Stevens's hair. Add straight and curving lines to the arms and body. In Congress Stevens fought to secure rights for the newly freed slaves.

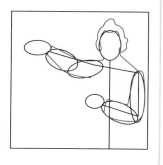

**4** Erase the guides for the top of the head and for the arms. Add straight lines for guides to make the eyes, nose, and mouth. Add curved lines for the jacket as shown.

**5** Inside the hand ovals, draw the details of the hands and fingers. Erase the guide for the body you made in step 1. Draw lines for the jacket and collar as shown.

**6** Add the eyes, eyebrows, nose, and mouth as shown. Erase the guides for the hands. Add curved lines for the piece of paper in Stevens's hand.

**7** Erase the guides you made for the face. Add circles to the eyes. Draw lines on the jacket sleeves. Add more lines to Stevens's shirt and tie as shown.

**8** Erase the guide that you made in step 1. Finish by shading the drawing. The jacket, hair, and tie are dark.

# The Death and the Legacy of Andrew Johnson

After the impeachment hearing, President Johnson served out the rest of his term. He knew he stood no chance at reelection. When Ulysses S. Grant won the 1868 election, Andrew Johnson left the White House with his family and went home to Tennessee in March 1869.

Johnson ran for the Senate in 1869 and for Congress in 1872, but he lost both times. In 1874, he successfully ran for the U.S. Senate and took office in 1875. Shortly after arriving in Washington D.C., Johnson visited his daughter and granddaughter. On this visit he suffered a series of strokes and died on July 31, 1875. Johnson's legacy has been mixed because of his impeachment and his actions during Reconstruction. However, Johnson supported the Constitution and the Union at a time when few other Southerners would. Johnson was hardworking and made an effort to learn what he never had a chance to study at school. This drive allowed Johnson to become the seventeenth U.S. president.

**1** Start your drawing of Andrew Johnson by making a large rectangle. Inside the rectangle draw two oval guides for the head and body. Draw a straight line to connect the head and body ovals.

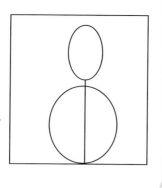

**2** Draw lines inside the head oval. These will be your guides for the eyes, nose, and mouth. Draw three slanted lines around the body oval. These will be guides for the arms and shoulders.

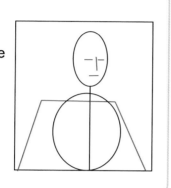

**3** Add wavy lines around the face for hair. Note how the hair line curves up near his left ear. Add lines around the slanted guides you made for Andrew Johnson's arms.

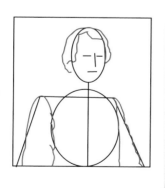

**4** Draw squiggly lines to connect the head and the body of Andrew Johnson. Add curved lines for the eyebrows, jaw, and chin as shown. Add a curved line for an ear.

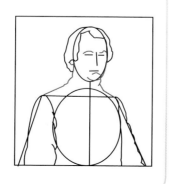

**5** Erase most of the head oval. Erase the body guides. Add wavy lines to the hair. Draw his eyes, nose, and mouth as shown. Add curved and straight lines for his shirt and jacket collar.

**6** Erase the guides for the face. Add circles to the eyes that you added in step 5. Add wavy lines to make the vest inside the jacket. Add shapes and lines to Johnson's collar and add a bow tie as shown.

**7** Add details to Andrew Johnson's ear and face as shown. Draw circles for the buttons on the vest and the jacket. Add more wavy lines for the folds and creases on the jacket and the vest.

**8** Erase the large rectangle that you made in step 1. Finish by shading the drawing. Shade the buttons dark. Make the folds in the jacket darker than the rest of the drawing.

# Timeline

**1808**   Andrew Johnson is born in Raleigh, North Carolina, on December 29.

**1822**   Johnson becomes an apprentice to a tailor named James Selby. An apprentice is a person who learns a trade from a more experienced person.

**1826**   Andrew Johnson and his family settle in Greeneville, Tennessee.

**1827**   Eliza McCardle and Andrew Johnson are married.

**1829**   Johnson is elected as an alderman in Greeneville, Tennessee.

**1835**   Andrew Johnson is elected mayor of Greeneville.

**1835–1843**   Johnson serves as a state representative and then as a state senator.

**1843–1853**   Andrew Johnson serves as U.S. congressman from Tennessee.

**1853–1857**   Johnson serves as the governor of Tennessee.

**1857**   Johnson is elected to the U.S. Senate.

**1861**   The Civil War begins on April 12.

**1862**   Abraham Lincoln appoints Andrew Johnson as the military governor of Tennessee.

**1864**   Johnson is elected U.S. vice president.

**1865**   The Civil War ends on April 9. Lincoln is assassinated on April 14. Johnson is sworn in as president on April 15.

**1867**   Johnson and the Senate approve the purchase of Alaska.

**1868**   Johnson is impeached by the U.S. House of Representatives on February 24. On May 16, the U.S. Senate finds Johnson innocent of the impeachment charges.

**1875**   Johnson is elected to the U.S. Senate. On July 31, Johnson dies after a series of strokes.

# Glossary

**alderman** (OL-der-men)  A member of a city or town lawmaking body that is elected by the people of that city or town.

**cabinet** (KAB-nit)  A group of people who advise important government officials.

**Civil War** (SIH-vul WOR)  The war fought between the Northern and the Southern states of America from 1861 to 1865.

**Confederate** (kun-FEH-duh-ret)  Relating to the Southern states that made up the Confederate States of America during the American Civil War.

**Congress** (KON-gres)  The part of the U.S. government that makes laws.

**defense** (dih-FENS)  Something that saves from harm.

**impeached** (im-PEECHD)  To have charged a government official with a crime.

**lawyers** (LOY-erz)  People who give advice about the law and who speak for people in court.

**legacy** (LEH-guh-see)  Something that has been handed down from another person.

**Monroe Doctrine** (mun-ROH DOK-trin)  A course of action that began in 1823 during the presidency of James Monroe. It limited the activity of European powers in North America and South America.

**nomination** (nah-muh-NAY-shun)  The suggestion that someone or something should be given a position.

**plantation** (plan-TAY-shun)  A very large farm where crops are grown.

**poverty** (PAH-ver-tee)  The state of being poor.

**Reconstruction** (ree-kun-STRUK-shun)  A period in U.S. history (1865–1877) after the Civil War when the Confederate states attempted to rebuild their economies.

**traitor** (TRAY-tur)  A person who turns against his or her country.

**treaty** (TREE-tee)  An official agreement, signed and agreed upon by each party.

**U.S. Constitution** (YOO ES kon-stih-TOO-shun)  The document adopted in 1788 that explains the different parts of the nation's government and how each part works.

**Whig Party** (HWIG PAR-tee)  Political party in the United States from 1834 to 1856 formed in opposition to the Democratic Party.

# Index

# Web Sites

Due to the changing nature of Internet links, PowerKids Press has developed an
online list of Web sites related to the subject of this book. This site is updated
regularly. Please use this link to access the list:
www.powerkidslinks.com/kgdpusa/ajohnson/